PRIMARY RESEARCH GROUP

Trends in Rare Book & Documents Special Collections Management

~ *2011 Edition* ~

TRENDS IN RARE BOOK & DOCUMENTS SPECIAL COLLECTIONS MANAGEMENT, 2011 EDITION

ISBN # 1-57440-164-5

TABLE OF CONTENTS

ABOUT THE AUTHOR

Joan Oleck is a Brooklyn, NY-based freelance journalist who has been on staff at BusinessWeek, Newsday, and the Detroit News and has contributed to publications such as Bloomberg News, Salon, and Parenting Magazine.

INTRODUCTION AND SUMMARY

This monograph profiles the management practices and other business decisions of nine high-profile special collections/rare book libraries. Included are The Fales Library and Special Collections of New York University; the Rosenbach Museum and Library in Philadelphia; the Lillian Goldman Law Library at Yale University; the Jewish Theological Seminary Library; the Thomas Fisher Rare Book Library at the University of Toronto; the Cushing Memorial Library and Archives at Texas A&M University in College Station; the Harry Ransom Center Research Library and Museum at the University of Texas in Austin; the American Museum of Natural History Library in New York City; and the Wisconsin Historical Society Library-Archives in Madison, Wisconsin..

Each library in this report is unique. The nine institutions differ in size (from the Lillian Goldman Law Library to the Harry Ransom Center). They differ in focus--from avant-garde culture (Fales), Jewish learning (JTS) and the law (Lillian Goldman); to natural history (AMNH) and social history (Wisconsin Historical Society).

The nine libraries also follow separate and distinct paths in how they celebrate and present humankind's towering intellectual and artistic achievements across a span of seven centuries. Some are university libraries (Texas A&M, Fales), one is a museum library (American Museum of Natural History) and one is the library of a state historical society. Two (the Rosenbach and the Harry Ransom Center) combine the museum-library functions.

Yet common threads exist. A dwindling amount of storage space and staff cuts due to budget constraints are frequent, unfortunately predictable complaints.

But beyond those evergreen issues is a more positive commonality: the libraries' large investment in time and budget to digitization of their archives. There is good reason for this move: Librarians recognize that digital technology is key to the preservation of their collections' fragile original materials. Digitization is also a publicity aid and a way to save paper and "go green."

Digitization

Several libraries reported major strides toward digitizing their collections and publications. "We don't subscribe to anything in print if there's an electronic version," an American Museum of Natural History's librarian said. Library users at AMNH in fact can now read materials online, on cell phones, and on electronic tablets. The natural history Library is also dealing with the limitations of electronic reading devices by experimenting with a new format called ePub that lets readers enlarge text on pdfs.

The Jewish Theological Society Library has already digitized nine separate collections available under a "Search the Digital Collections" link off its home page. And Harry Ransom Center's librarian estimates it's thus far amassed 500,000 digitized images.

Other libraries, such as NYU's Fales and Cushing at Texas A&M, are just starting digitization, with deliberate caution to ensure good planning. "We like our digitized materials to be very rich for researchers from off site," a Rosenbach librarian said, explaining why that institution is proceeding slowly. Some libraries also reported delays due to the technical processes and training involved in digitization, plus the time needed for librarians to prepare the metadata that makes digital search possible.

Digitization however can increase collection use. The Thomas Fisher Library reported that after posting its research presentation, *The Discovery and Early Development of Insulin* online, "The American Diabetes Society downloaded the whole thing about a half hour after we put it up." This same librarian said that online information is attracting extra users. "The more information that is available and [the more that] even digital images— surrogates—are out there online, the more people want to see the original and use it," he said.

Digitization has prompted a number of partnerships and consortiums. AMNH has become a member of the Biodiversity Heritage, a group of natural history libraries in the U.S. and U.K. aiming to create digitized versions of all literature about living organisms. AMNH also works with the Internet Archive to scan its books for digitization. JTS, meanwhile, has partnered with Hebrewbooks.org, a not-for-profit that focuses on digitizing rare books, especially rabbinic texts. Another partner is the Digital Scriptorium, a project run by the University of California-Berkley that focuses on pre-1540 manuscripts. The Rosenbach is partnering with the national library of Israel to transform Hebrew manuscripts, and with the University of Manchester to digitize Chaucer materials. Texas A&M is using digitization to increase access to its materials for other institutions in the Texas A&M university system. And the Library-Archives of the Wisconsin Historical Society is part of a three-way partnership with the University of Wisconsin and Google to digitize the state's enormous trove of state and national historic material.

An obvious benefit of digitization is the ease it allows patrons to copy images on site. Harry Ransom's librarian said his institution already had moved away from photocopying. Libraries like AMNH and Thomas Fisher described state-of-the-art scanners that simultaneously copy and produce digital images for downloading onto thumb drives.

Digitization can also produce profits: The Library-Archives in Wisconsin has an active historic photo e-commerce business in operation as well as a genealogical records business; for a fee, patrons can browse and order photos and various documents online and receive them online or by mail.

Security

While the American Museum of Natural History described biometric security features, which can scan the iris or fingerprints, other libraries said they still depend on cameras

(Lillian Goldman), motion detectors (Thomas Fisher) or good old-fashioned eagle-eyed librarians.

Harry Ranson and Texas A&M both use the new Aeon system, which tracks circulation materials and allows patrons not only to request materials but to track their personal records of use.

Patrons' cameras have become an issue, as more and more people use their cell phones' photography feature. "We've kind of given up to a certain extent," NYU Fales' librarian said. "We've actually found that it's easier to let them use their handheld than have them ask for photocopies."

Cell phones, he added, do "less damage and the quality of the image [patrons are] going to get is so poor they can't reproduce it."

Harry Ransom is just starting to allow patrons to use cameras this spring. "We decided we were out of step with the rest of the world," the librarian said, conceding that there's really no way to police patrons from putting copyrighted and rare materials up on the web.

Outreach and Fund-raising

Social media are playing an increasing role in helping research libraries get the word out. A number of libraries described blogs, RSS feeds and Twitter accounts. To publicize its ongoing Civil War sesquicentennial observance Rosenbach, on its blog, is using an installment technique—much like an old-fashioned novel released chapter by chapter. Items change almost daily along the lines of "what historic Civil War event happened exactly 150 years ago today?"

Lillian Goldman captures images of its exhibits in its blogs, and Fales posts videos of its series "Critical Topics in Foods" online. Rosenbach successfully used Groupon, the discount coupon website. Its Groupon effort offered discounted tickets to a tour. The library-museum got more than 700 responders within 48 hours—with many of those responders first-time visitors.

Other unusual outreach projects include one from Cushing at Texas A& E, where each year, the public is invited to a workshop to create a physical book, making the paper and setting the type on a replica of the English Common Press. AMNH's special collections librarian is considering an "adopt a book" offer so that regular donors can help repair those Library volumes most in need of preservation.

Preservation

Under the preservation category, the Lillian Goldman library is using "boxing and enclosures" to preserve on a budget. Acid-free envelopes, pamphlet binders, and other items from a company called Custom Manufacturing, Inc. cut down on conservation costs. Especially helpful are the company's MicroClimate acid-free boxes" dubbed "pizza boxes."

At Harry Ranson, a particularly unusual feature is a mold removal chamber, offering a special exhaust feature to protect workers

THE UNIVERSITY OF TORONTO, CANADA'S THOMAS FISHER RARE BOOK LIBRARY

We spoke to Richard Landon, director of the Thomas Fisher Rare Book Library and a professor of English at the University of Toronto. Landon has been with the library for 44 years.

General Description

The University of Toronto was founded in 1827 and began to expand about 1850. But in 1890 came a turning point: University College, containing the library, burned. That's why all university collections today date back to1890. That was the year of the devastating fire, of course. But it also was the year when institutions across North America, Britain, and Europe rallied around the burned college and donated enough materials to restore U-T's collection to its previous level of excellence.

Today, the University of Toronto has over 70,000 students on three campuses and is a research-oriented institution, with graduate studies in almost every field.

Located on the main St. George, campus is the Thomas Fisher Rare Book Library, named in honor of Thomas Fisher. Fisher (1792-1874), emigrated from Yorkshire to Upper Canada's Humber River region in 1821, where he operated a grist mill and was active in the public life of the community. In 1973 his great-grandsons, Sidney and Charles Fisher, donated to the library their collections of Shakespeare, various 20th century authors, and etchings of the 17th century Bohemian artist Wenceslaus Hollar.

The Department of Rare Books and Special Collections was founded in November 1955, when a special librarian was hired to pull together medieval manuscripts and other rare materials that had begun to accumulate.

The Fisher Library now has its own building: an impressive structure with a five-story tower surrounded by five galleries that run around its perimeter. The library is attached to the university's main Robarts Library, which in turn contains about 40 different libraries under its purview. Each college also has its own library, and all of those smaller libraries have multiple collections, some quite famous: Trinity College's collection focuses on the Anglican Church; St. Michael's College focuses on medieval studies.

The Fisher, which is separate, and employs about 18 full-time staffers plus part-time graduate students, houses the university's central rare books department as well as the university archives. In sum, the collection is devoted to the giants of British, European, and Canadian literature and art and to the history of science and medicine.

The collection is large, containing 700,000 volumes and 2,500 linear meters of manuscript holdings, Fisher is particularly known for its Shakespearean-Elizabethan holdings, but: "Literally we have 2,000 BC cuneiforms up to Margaret Atwood, so we span a huge [time frame] and reflect virtually every field in between," Landon says. "There are over 300 special collections…what we have on display ranges from an 11th century Greek New Testament from Constantinople to a pop-up Bible from last year.

The library is also proud of its first edition of the King James Bible, the focus of a current exhibit on the English language Bible.

Acquisitions and Development

Fisher relies on a development staffer who is with the Robarts Library and the central library system. Landon also says he calls on a very active "Friends of" organization. But, "I'm the one who hustles the bucks," the librarian adds, describing contacts and people he regularly calls on for targeted donations. The Fisher has been fortunate in terms of bequests, Landon says, but "patience is a virtue." He's lined up four or five estates but has no idea of when or how much those sources may contribute.

Meanwhile, as part of a publicly funded university, the Fisher and its endowment enjoys relative stability and less exposure than private universities suffer Altogether, the Fisher's endowment is about $3 million, Landon says. He also describes acquisition funds endowed for Canadiana manuscripts plus funding for Italian materials, including Italian Rima poetry that extend from the medieval period to the 18th century.

Procurement and Purchasing

The Fisher has long-time relationships with booksellers and auction houses. "Because I've been around so long, I have dealers I've been dealing with for 40 years," Landon says. "I get quoted stuff every day," before materials are listed in catalogues.

Private gifts also come in regularly. "Canada has very advantageous tax laws in terms of [giving] tax receipts for gifts in kind. So we get quite a lot that way," Landon says. "We get huge masses of writers' papers, especially Canadian novelists, playwrights, and poets—that's one of our specialties." Writers get a tax write-off for donating their materials. Big names whose materials are at the library include Margaret Atwood, Leonard Cohen, Lawrence Hill, and Earle Birney.

The library requires legal possession of the materials it accepts; rights remain with the writer or estate.

Security

The library has a full security system with motion detectors, Landon says. Patron's cameras are allowed, under supervision.

Even better than cameras is the library's first-class scanner, where patrons can plug in a thumb drive, download an image, and email the results to themselves. Patrons are permitted to handle the books themselves, again under supervision.

Digitization

The library has been active in digitization for ten years. It has six major projects which it initiated. The most popular project is on the discovery of insulin, which occurred in 1922 at the University of Toronto. The papers of Nobel Prize winner Sir Frederick Banting and Dr. Charles Best and their fellow insulin discoverers are housed at the Fisher; the library recently loaned its diabetes-related materials for an exhibit at the New York Historical Society. The materials also appear at a separate website, *The Discovery and Early Development of Insulin*, which links to the library's website. "The American Diabetes Society downloaded the whole thing about a half hour after we put it up," says Landon.

Another digital project and separate website that the librarian calls "spectacular" is titled *Anatomia* and includes five thousand anatomical images. A third, *The Barren Lands*, concerns exploration of the Arctic and is based on a manuscript collection.

"We have a whole bunch more [projects] ready to go," Landon says. "IT [information technology] is what's holding us up." The main library's information technology department carries out the digital work—creating the metadata, or what Landon as a librarian views as indexing. And this can be time-consuming. For *Anatomia*, for instance, an anatomy expert had to be hired so that patrons could eventually type in the name of a particular bone and obtain images and information from the website's database. "What [the site] has is a level of indexing that will search images according to words," Landon says.

On digitization overall, "We'd like to be further along than we are," Landon says. "The problem of the financing always is that it's not so hard to find money for science-based projects; it was easy to find money for *Insulin*. But for humanities projects, it's a lot harder. Funders include foundations in the United States, such as the Gladys Krieble Delmas Foundation of New York, which has helped out on digitization of the *Barren Lands* material and materials related to the 17th century etchings of Wenceslas Hollar. Hollar is famous for the views he created of London before and after its devastating fire of 1666.

Outreach and Publicity

The Fisher Library has a full-time publicist on staff, who handles its outreach publicity for the institution's three exhibitions a year, each with its own catalogue. Toronto has four daily newspapers, which exponentially multiplies the library's publicity for exhibits. Recent such events have included the current exhibit on the English Bible and the 200th anniversary of Charles Darwin's birth in 2009. The latter made a splash for displaying a major find by Landon: a previously unknown and unpublished letter from Darwin to Charles Kingsley, the British clergyman who famously and infamously wrote the didactic children's fairy tale *The Water-Babies*.

Twice a year the library publishes a newsletter, *Halcyon*, which is widely distributed; and makes its exhibition openings big events. "We had a huge opening for the Bible exhibition, including the Archbishop of Toronto, Landon says.

The Fisher Library has also loaned materials to such institutions as the Royal Ontario Museum and the New York Historical Society and keeps a close connection to the teaching activities of the university, with visits by classes "almost on a daily basis."

The public is welcome to visit the library at any time.

Meetings

Landon belongs to multiple organizations and has been active in the Rare Books and Manuscripts section of the American Library Association as well as the International Federation of Library Association's Rare Books and Manuscripts section, which he chaired for several years. He is a member of the Grolier Club and the bibliographic societies of America, London, and Canada.

He is also active in the English Short Title Catalogue Project to create a machine-readable union catalogue of English books and pamphlets. Originally limited to the 18th century the project now dates back to 1473.

Preservation

The Fisher Library has its own conservation laboratory and a professional conservator who mounts the institution's exhibitions. "We need far more, of course; conservation is ongoing and changes all the time; priorities change," Landon says. Once the library agrees to a loan or plans to exhibit a particular manuscript or artwork, in-house repairs are the first step.

Most work is done on-site but binding work is outsourced. The Royal Ontario Museum has done conservation work for the Fisher Library without charge.

One factor about the library that Landon emphasizes is the increasing use of its collections. "We're being used more and more because, ironically the more information that is available and [the more that] even digital images—surrogates—are out there online, the more people want to see the original and use it," Landon says. "We are primarily a research institution, and most of the researchers who come here are either faculty or graduate students…[but] we have people coming from all over the world because we have things no one else has."

LILLIAN GOLDMAN LAW LIBRARY AT YALE UNIVERSITY, NEW HAVEN

We spoke to Mike Widener, rare book librarian, who has been with the library since 2006 and previously headed Special Collections at the Tarlton Law Library at the University of Texas-Austin.

General Description

The Rare Book Collection that Widener oversees is housed within the Lillian Goldman Law Library, named for its 1990s benefactor. Lillian Goldman library, in turn, is housed at the Yale Law School on the university campus.

Yale, of course, is a top-ranked institution that traces its roots back to the 1640s when colonial clergyman established the then-college in order to continue the tradition of European liberal education in the New World. In 1701 a charter was granted and in 1718 the name Yale College established in honor of the local merchant who gave the institution 417 books, funding, and a portrait of King George I. In the 1930s a system of residential colleges modeled after those of Cambridge and Oxford in Britain was established.

Since then Yale has expanded to a university of 11,560 students and a 3,695-member faculty. The campus is home to the undergraduate school of Yale College, the Graduate School of Arts and Sciences, and 13 professional schools.

The law library became part of Yale Law School in 1845 when the school that originally had housed it lost its one and only faculty member, spurring concern among New Haven's lawyers that they might lose this treasured resource.

Today's Lillian Goldman Law Library Rare Book Collection is not part of the university library system, centered at Sterling Memorial Library, nor is it connected to the Beineke Rare Book and Manuscript Library. Instead, the Rare Book Collection reports to the dean of the law school and is located in the law library, which in turn occupies the law school's top three floors plus three basement levels.

Located in the law library's Paskus-Danziger Rare Book Room, the Rare Book Collection is rich in centuries-old Anglo-American common law materials, including case reports, digests, legal statutes, treatises, and popular works on the law. Among its treasures is the William Blackstone Collection, the world's largest, most comprehensive collection of the works of Sir William Blackstone. This 18th century author is best known for his *Commentaries on the Laws of England*—considered to be the most influential book on the common law tradition.

Other rare works in the collection include the 1,600-volume Roman-Canon Law Collection of the Association of the Bar of the City of New York; 800 volumes of Italian municipal statutes from the 14th to 19th centuries, contained within 800 printed volumes and 55 manuscripts; the law libraries of Lewis Morris, a Declaration of Independence signee; and legal manuscripts spanning the 12th to the 20th centuries and comprising medieval treatises, English law reports, early American lawyers' account books, and 19th century student notebooks from the law schools at Yale, Columbia, and Litchfield, Connecticut (the nation's first law school).

A recent addition to the Lillian Goldman collection is the whimsically titled Juvenile Jurisprudence Collection, containing more than 200 law-related children's books donated by the late professor emeritus, Morris L. Cohen.

According to Widener, "There are not that many academic law libraries that have substantial collections of rare books, manuscripts, or archives; it's a minority." (Others in that minority include the law libraries at Harvard, George Washington, the University of Minnesota, Tarleton at the University of Texas, and the University of California-Berkeley.)

The Rare Book Collection has just one staffer—Widener—since the recession-battered Yale endowment "took a big hit," forcing the elimination of the collection's staff assistant. In total the collection's holdings comprise 50,000 volumes as well as about 1,000 volumes of manuscript materials—though, because of space limitations, the collection does not accept whole "papers of" collections from famous jurists or other legal scholars (Sterling Memorial houses such materials.).

Along with books and manuscripts, the Rare Book Collection has recently become the repository—"and we're quite proud of it," Widener quips—of Supreme Court bobblehead dolls—depicting justices throughout recent history, from Louis Brandeis to Sandra Day O'Connor. The dolls, which sell on eBay for up to $1,000, were obtained through a partnership with *Green Bag*, a journal devoted to scholarly legal writing—and tongue-in-cheek entertainment. How did the bobbleheads come to the library? "We asked," Widener says. "No one else ever asked."

Acquisitions and Development

The Rare Book Collection works with the law school's development office to pay for raise funds for acquisitions. The collection also has two small endowed funds of its own for this purpose plus an annual allotment from the library's general acquisition fund. The law library has other endowed book funds which at times are put at the Rare Book Collection's disposal.

In addition the collection has contacts with two angel-donors who at times give Widener money to buy certain books. He established relationships with both donors during his time at the University of Texas.

Procurement and Purchasing

Widener works with rare book dealers frequently; and most acquisitions are made through this route, with occasional other purchases at auction. The librarian says he prefers to see what the dealers offer first—before they put those materials in their catalogues—to distributing wish lists.

Estates are other sources for materials, and the librarian says he makes a point of letting people down easy, making suggestions where collections might go if they are inappropriate for the Rare Book Collection.

Donations that are accepted must be a "flat-out gift" with no conditions. Copyright is rarely an issue because of the materials' age.

Security

Laptops and pencils are allowed in the library. "I actually encourage digital cameras," Widener adds. "I tell people, 'You can take all of the pictures you want.'" As a one-person operation he can't police cameras, he says, and, besides, the images being reproduced are not good enough for publication.

For researchers needing publication-quality images, Widener personally carries the source volume to Yale's Photo and Design Services, works with the photographer to prevent damage, then carries the volume back. A charge is requested for such work but brings in no real revenue. Researchers purchasing images, however, are required to cite the collection and provide a copy of the eventual publication.

For security against theft, the reading room is always locked; nothing may leave the room; and a required form includes each researcher's identity and signed pledge to abide by the rules.

Digitization

"We've done some," Widener says, "and for the library as a whole we have what's called a Digital Initiatives Task Force"; he serves as a member. He already has digitized about a half dozen large manuscripts requested by patrons. "Now we're looking for ways to actually deliver those to the public."

Widener says he is currently ironing out the technical issues of digitization, the design of the website, and the best way to build a coherent collection of digital materials. One idea is to digitize materials about the law school—its printed catalogues and yearbooks. However, "We have to cut it off [by date] fairly early because there are privacy concerns about people who are living and not wanting their yearbook photos on the web, but there are some older things that would be valuable." Another digital project: A current faculty member at the law school is interested in digitizing an early printed edition of the *Corpus Juris Canonici* [*Body of Canon Law*]. These manuscripts contain early medieval, fundamental works of canon law.

Yet a third proposed project aims to digitize student notebooks from the Litchfield Law School. Litchfield, Connecticut was the site of the first law school in the United States—a stand-alone school that lasted until the 1830s. The Yale law school Rare Book Collection has the largest collection of these notebooks, dating back to 1799 and a trove of details about law lectures at that time.

An interesting historic anecdote about Litchfield from Widener: "Aaron Burr was a student there."

Outreach and Publicity

Widener has started the Yale Library Rare Book Blog and readership is strong. He writes about acquisitions, special events, and accounts of university classes that come in to look at the books. Since Widener has been with the library, a state-of-the-art exhibits room has been built and has hosted about a half dozen exhibits. Widener captures images of the exhibit items, writes captions, and puts them up in installments on the Rare Book Blog.

He is also looking at the possibility of creating separate web sites for the exhibits.

An exhibit that was up at the time of the interview was a partnership with the Elizabethan Club of Yale, an exclusive literary society celebrating its centennial this year. The club has its own rare book collection, including a First Folio from William Shakespeare. The library exhibit, titled "Life and Law and Early Modern England," describes the role the law played during the time of Queen Elizabeth I and the early Stuarts. Included in the exhibit, also featured on the blog, was an early legal treatise about the right of Mary, Queen of Scots, to succeed Elizabeth. Also included: "law for the laymen" style practitioners' books; justice of the peace manuals; writings by Francis Bacon; and a masque—or play—that took place at one of the Inns of Court, or British legal societies, where Shakespeare is believed to have performed.

Past exhibits have included the bobblehead jurists and what Widener calls "a great example of outreach": 20 law books that have medieval manuscripts as part of their vellum bindings because Renaissance era book binders cut them up to use for law books. In fact the oldest item in the Rare Book Collection is a bound book's "paste-down" containing a fragment of a religious manuscript over 1,000 years old.

The latter exhibit happened in conjunction with a meeting at Yale of the Medieval Academy of America, which includes leading medievalists from the United States and

Europe. Conference attendees toured the collection and were able to identify the fragments' origins right on the spot. "They were like kids, with their iPhones out," Widener recalls. "We got so much good information. It was very gratifying."

Meetings

Widener regularly attends the Associations of American Law Libraries' annual meeting. That group in turn has a rare books special interest section. He also occasionally attends meetings of the Rare Books and Manuscript Section of the American Library Association and the American Society for Legal History.

Preservation

Widener misses the assistant he lost due to budget cuts because the assistant possessed preservation skills. Now Widener is concentrating on using "boxing and enclosures" for conservation. This entails buying acid-free envelopes, pamphlet binders, and other items from a company called Custom Manufacturing, Inc.

Especially helpful are the company's MicroClimate acid-free boxes" dubbed "pizza boxes" in the library sphere. Books are measured precisely and the company sends specially cut cardboard which fits around the volume. "It makes an inexpensive but very effective enclosure."

The library has no facilities so Widener occasionally uses outside conservators to repair damaged items, but is limited by budgetary constraints.

"I'm not a big fan of intervention," Widener admits, "because the evidence of [the collected materials'] original structure is really important. 'Less is more.'"

THE JEWISH THEOLOGICAL SEMINARY LIBRARY

We spoke to Naomi Steinberger, director of library services. She has been at JTS for 23 years.

General Description

The Jewish Theological Seminary (JTS), in New York, traces its roots to 1886 and the efforts of rabbis Dr. Sabato Morais and Dr. H. Pereira Mendes, plus lay leaders from Sephardic congregations in Philadelphia and New York. The seminary's stated mission is to preserve the knowledge and practice of historical Judaism. In 1887, JTS held its first class in the vestry of the Spanish-Portuguese Synagogue, New York City's oldest congregation. Today, JTS maintains a full campus on New York's Upper West Side.

JTS is a full-scale Jewish university granting degrees at all levels through diverse schools: The Graduate School; The Rabbinical School; H. L. Miller Cantorial School and College of Jewish Music; William the Davidson Graduate School of Jewish Education; Albert A. List College of Jewish Studies; and the Rebecca and Israel Ivry Prozdor High School.

Also offered through JTS are five research institutes and enrichment programs for the Jewish community in the United States, Israel, and worldwide.

Central to JTS's aim to enhance the scholarly ambiance of its community of learning and make Judaism come alive for new generations is the Library, acknowledged as the largest trove of Hebrew manuscripts in the world—totaling 11,000 Hebrew codices (manuscript volumes).

A devastating fire in April 1966 destroyed or damaged 70,000 volumes in the library, but its oldest books and manuscripts fortunately were spared.

Overall, the library today holds 400,000 volumes; 600 marriage contracts, or *ketubot*; 250 scrolls; and 2,000 linear feet of archives; plus 35,000 *geniza* fragments found in Cairo at the end of the 19th century. These range from the tenth to the 19th century. "They're really a window into the cultural life and historical life in the Middle East over ten centuries," Steinberger says. JTS's *geniza* collection is the second largest in the world, after Cambridge University.

Geniza or *genizah* (*genizot* in the plural) is the Hebrew word for the storeroom or other depository in a Jewish synagogue or cemetery that holds aging-out Hebrew-language books and papers awaiting burial. The reason for burial? Jewish law forbids discarding writings, religious or secular, that contain the name of God. "That really is the source of the Cairo *geniza*," Steinberger says, "because they never buried the material and the world has been really lucky that they just stuffed it in this attic for a thousand years and never dealt with it."

This tradition lives on at JTS: Today, even photocopies of holy texts may be discarded only in special receptacles, from where they are sent out for burial.

Such details some lead observers to believe that JTS's library holdings are all ancient. But Steinberger is anxious to emphasize the institution's contemporary collections in Jewish studies and culture, as well. Materials range from sound recordings, moving images, e-books and graphic arts pieces to an extensive postcard collection. "It's all integrated in our library," Steinberger says. "We have a separate reading room for special collections and they're shelved in a different area, but our catalogue is integrated."

On staff are 15 librarians and ten non-librarians, who include subject specialists in Jewish music, Jewish art, and conservation.

Acquisitions and Development

JTS's library relies on the overall institution's development staff. The library has legacy gifts for the acquisition of rare books and manuscripts—"but not a lot," Steinberger says. "We haven't been acquiring as much now as we used to." The library also has a book endowment for contemporary material—fed by private donations and foundations—that currently stands at $475,000.

The library has a paid membership status that allows members to borrow books and attend special events. Outsiders may take advantage of the library's open access policy at any time.

A new archive just processed contains audio recordings and documents from Rabbi Judah Nadich, President Dwight D/ Eisenhower's chaplain who was present at the liberation of the World War II concentration camps.

Procurement and Purchases

The library maintains relationships with book dealers and purchases general collections. Recently, it had a gift of a trove of rare books, and it has received archival collections as legacies or gifts. Terms for gifts include the requirement of complete control by the library. Copyright issues are rare given the age of most materials.

In the early 1990s, with the fall of the Soviet Union, the library made a distinct effort to purchase records from towns in Eastern Europe near the sites of once-thriving Jewish communities, Steinberger says.

While the library prides itself on making its materials available at no cost, some revenue is obtained by the sale of catalogs at exhibits, the publication of library materials by for-profit ventures, and admission fees to special events like concerts.

Security

People coming in to use the special collections must make an appointment, specifying what they need the librarians to have ready. They can bring pencils and laptops but not cell phones.

For photography, "We're experimenting with that," Steinberger says. "In theory we're saying people can take photographs. In practice we're finding it a little more difficult because [we can offer] only certain types of material under certain conditions. If they want two or three images for their own personal use to go home and work on something, we prefer that they give it to us and we'll digitize it and send it to them."

Digitization

JTS is already far along in its digitization process, with nine separate collections categories already available under a "Search the Digital Collections" link off its home page. Those categories include: Archives; 700 Jewish Wedding documents (*ketubot* and poems); 450 Judaica America news clippings and pamphlets; 100 Music Collections (scores); 89 Rare Books; 2,500 Bookplates; JTS Student Theses; Selected Hebrew Manuscripts (and other materials); and 2,000 portraits from the late 19th century into the mid-20th century.

"We've been digitizing for about ten years," Steinberger reports. "We're working on it constantly; we don't have enough staff or money to do more, but we're working hard." A digital assets management system—a catalogue—was put up in 2007, she says, and future plans call for a new digitized Manuscripts category initially containing 80 items plus the digitization of the library's early 20th century postcard collection—extending Jewish New Year's greetings and showing views of the Holy Land Eastern as well as European synagogues that no longer exist.

Digitization items are available as non-searchable pdfs. A partner in the process is Hebrewbooks.org, a not-for-profit that focuses on digitizing rare books, especially rabbinic texts as well as JTS's library's own manuscript microfilms. Currently, Hebrewbooks.org links to JTS's library website dialogue is underway about creating a link back from JTS.

Other partners include Digital Scriptorium, a project run by the University of California-Berkley focusing on pre-1540 manuscripts; and the Friedberg Genizah Project, which seeks to digitize all 200,000 fragments belonging to the Cairo trove.

Publicity and Outreach

The library conducts an open house twice a year, with the next one scheduled for June 1, 2011. It is just completing a video about its offerings, which will posted on the website. Also available on the site is a reference blog—about the special or general collections—on which researchers may post questions for the reference materials.

Another feature is book talks by faculty members and publicity about exhibits including the new one about marriage contract *ketubot*. Loans to other libraries are yet another form of publicity.

Outreach to New York's Jewish community includes tours for synagogue and Jewish school groups, as well as a "Parsha Partnership" bringing bar and bat mitvah students into the library to look at early printed manuscripts for their individual portions of Torah (the Hebrew Bible) readings.

Exhibits

"Because we're uptown [at 122nd Street and Broadway] and not midtown, it's hard to get people to come here for exhibits, s that was one of the impetuses for having an exhibit of ketubbot at the Jewish Museum," Steinberger says. Smaller exhibits are featured at the JTS library; a recent one focused on the restoration of a 14th century *haggadah*, the book read as part of the Pesach, or Passover ritual. "We're not doing as many on-site exhibits now, because we feel it doesn't have as much of an impact," the librarian explains.

Meetings

Steinberger is involved in the Ex Libris library community, the vendor for many of JTS's digitization efforts. She is also active in the Association for Jewish Libraries and the New York area theological libraries' association. The library's senior conservator also attends the American Institute of Conservation meetings.

Preservation

JTS's library has a full conservation lab on site, established in 1989 and expanded in 2001 with an Andrew W. Mellon Foundation grant. The lab is fully equipped and staffed by one-and-a-half staffers plus outside contract conservators. All binding work is outsourced.

In 2002, the Dr. Bernard Heller Foundation awarded another grant to the library for the full conservation of one of its most treasured manuscripts, *The Prato Haggadah.*

The spiritual significance of such items, which goes beyond their historic value, is central to the JTS library. "I do think we have an incredible cultural respect for the books and the history of them," Steinberger says. "Each one tells a story of the Jewish experience [and how diverse members of the Jewish community] ended up in New York, which always amazes me. They came from the four corners of the earth.'

"Every book tells about our cultural history."

NEW YORK UNIVERSITY, THE FALES LIBRARY & SPECIAL COLLECTIONS

We spoke to Head Librarian Marvin Taylor, who has been with Fales since 1993.

General Description

New York University, founded in 1831 by Albert Gallatin, the Treasury secretary to U.S. presidents Thomas Jefferson and James Madison, is today the nation's largest private research university. Its two portal campuses are in New York's Greenwich Village and the growing Middle East city of Abu Dhabi. NYU today offers 4,500 courses through 13 schools, colleges, and divisions.

The university's main library, Bobst Library, at Washington Square, which opened in 1973, houses the Fales Library and Special Collections.

History and Scope of Fales Library's Collections

The Fales Manuscript Collection was a gift to NYU in 1957 by DeCoursey Fales in memory of his father, Haliburton Fales. It is especially strong in English literature from the middle of the 18th century to the present, documenting developments in the novel. The collection is mostly from the Victorian and Edwardian period but also includes holdings from Sir Walter Scott, E.L. Doctorow, M. L. Rosenthal, Jerome Charyn, and Elizabeth Robins.

The Downtown Collection, which began in 1993, documents the downtown arts scene that evolved in SoHo and the Lower East Side from the 1970s through the early 1990s. That period's explosion of artistic creativity challenged and changed traditional literature, music, theater, performance, film, activism, dance, photography, video, and other art practices. The Downtown Collection is rich in archival holdings, including extensive film and video objects.

The Food and Cookery Collection is rapidly expanding its collection of books and manuscripts documenting food and food culture with a particular emphasis on New York City. Renowned food writer and NYU Professor Marion Nestle was instrumental in building this collection, Fales Librarian Marvin Taylor says.

Special collections include The Alfred C. Berol Collection of Lewis Carroll—the third largest collection of Lewis Carroll materials in the world; the Robert Frost Library, containing 2,000 volumes owned by the poet; the Kaplan and Rosenthal Judaica/Hebraica collections; the Erich Maria Remarque Library; and more.

Library Dimensions and Background

The Fales Library includes 225,000 volumes, and about 11,000 linear feet of manuscripts. There are also 30,000 sound recordings, 28,000 video recordings, and 8,000 film elements, according to Taylor. The library's four main categories include: the Fales Collection of rare books and manuscripts in English and American literature, the Downtown Collection, the Food and Cookery Collection and the general Special Collections of the NYU Libraries.

The library has four full-time curators and 3.5 FTE librarians. "It's not nearly sufficient for a collection of our size," Taylor says. "We're roughly the size of Emory or UC-San Diego and both have staffs that are twice our side. It's typical of New York that most cultural institutions are under-staffed."

Acquisitions and Development

The library shares a development person with the general libraries. Taylor oversees gifts in kind.

The Fales Library has an overall endowment plus smaller endowments, such as that for the Lewis Carroll Collection, artists' books, and other projects. All total, Taylor has about $70,000 a year to spend from endowment income. He also receives general library budget funding.

Gifts are in another category: "Gifts are funny," Taylor says. "We do keep track of them but they aren't counted by development any longer—in terms of being added into the amount raised each year." Last year, he says, the library acquired 783 linear feet of archives and very recently received a collection of 21,000 books from the Georg and Jenifer Lang collection. In eight years the library's food studies holdings have grown from zero to 55,000 volumes—becoming the largest food studies collection in the country.

The general libraries have a "friends of" group but Taylor says he ended the one for Fales, because "they're more trouble than they're worth."

For procurement, the library has relationships with book dealers, acquiring about 1,800 historical titles a year from dealers both in the United States and Britain. Donations from estates are a "constant" occurrence, Taylor says. Last year, 7,000 volumes were acquired this way. One particular recent prize was the Sylvester Manor Archive, named for a provisional plantation on New York State's Shelter Island in Long Island Sound. The plantation was founded in the 1630s. "And we were given the archive. It's amazing," Taylor says. "There's the early charter from the king; there are early maps of Shelter Island and Long Island. There are a lot of Dutch documents signed by chiefs of some of the native tribes on Long Island. It's a wonderful collection."

The library is also particularly strong in post 1970 art and has received several major donations including the Artists Space archive. This was the first Outsider gallery space in the United States, and hosted the art of avant-garde artists like Jean-Michele Basquiat, Kiki Smith, and Cindy Sherman.

Terms for gifts include a standard form for gifts—a letter of agreement. One thing the library does not ask for, Taylor says, is copyright. "I believe the artist should retain their copyright."

Security

Security is an important issue at Fales. "We have the reading room set up as best we can so that whoever is monitoring the room can see onto the tops of tables at all times," Taylor says. "We have a security system, including cameras and glass-break alarms. We also have the standard door alarms…the alarm is set off both at the security desk here in the library and at the security desk over at Central Security."

Standard security rules apply at Fales: patrons must check their bags and may use only pencils. Photo duplication has to be approved, and customers must clear permissions themselves first. "Everything goes up on the net instantly these days," Taylor says.

Cell phones also are not allowed. On cell phone cameras, "We've kind of given up to a certain extent. We have to approve the use of their cameras but we've actually found that it's easier to let them use their handheld than have them ask for photocopies. It does less damage and the quality of the image they're going to get is so poor they can't reproduce it." Cell phone cameras are not allowed for items under copyright.

In terms of actual security breaches, "I don't know that we've had any; I've been here 18 years and there are a couple of things I can't find but there aren't very many. I have a feeling they never made it to this building when the collections were moved many years ago."

Digitization

Fales is doing "very little" with digitization, Taylor says, though "it's taken off in the past year more than ever before.

"We're looking at digitization of parts of the Downtown Collection that are highly requested," Taylor said. "This is material that is being requested globally; we need to make it accessible on the net." The library's Judson Memorial Dance Theater records for instance comprise the single most requested collection. That dance troupe is credited with founding postmodern dance between 1962 and 1964.

The Downtown Collection includes not only postmodern dance but punk rock music, experimental fiction, and experimental music—"anything that happened below 14th Street that had to do with experimental work in the arts." That means Richard Hell and the Voidroids, Patti Smith, the Ramones, and more.

Very little other than finding aids has gone up onto the library's website. "We've put our energies into processing the collections instead of having lots of bells and whites on the website. It's not a very good website; we know that," Taylor says.

In terms of appealing to today's digitally-savvy youth, "I want to show the continuum of media so I can show them [materials ranging from] from [ancient Egyptian] cuneiform tablets up through moving image and digital materials—the similarities of media," Taylor said.

Outreach and Publicity

Fales knows its young users enough to have created a Facebook page that announces events and newly donated collections. "We do a ton of events every year. We do an ongoing series called "Critical Topics in Food," comprising three events a year all of which become videos posted online at NYU-TV's site about Fales. The library tries to tape all lectures, panels, and other events for similar distribution via the website. A recent such event, Taylor says, was "Postgender Food Writing," examining such issues as whether women are the only food writers anymore and which gender food manufacturers are targeting most.

For general publicity Fales gets assistance from the university's publicists—Taylor is currently hoping for a *New York Times* write-up about the Lang collection donation. He says he often reaches out to reporters about exhibitions and in the past year was pleased to see two reviews by *Times* critic Holland Cotter.

Users outside the university get their information through "the university's public relations machine," but Fales has also enjoyed coverage by the weekly calendar listings publication *Time Out*. "We're pretty much doing away with snail mail; our mailing list is about 3,000 people. We're sending out email invitations to these."

Outreach to teachers and faculty is another means for publicity, Taylor says. "We teach a lot of classes here"; last year 3,000 students came through for just this purpose. Classes offer students a chance to view and hear the library's displays of historic, performance-based, and gender studies-based archival materials.

Exhibits

The library has a gallery and hosts three exhibits a year using its own materials. One particularly successful exhibit was "You Make Me Feel Mighty Real," featuring the work of Robert Blanchon, the late queer conceptual photographer. The library worked with conceptual aids and Blanchon's estate to both display his work and document his life. More than 250 people attended the November 2009 opening.

Fales also reaches out to other libraries and galleries, offering items from its collection. One of those loans ended up as a new event. David Wojnarowicz was a conceptual artist in New York in the 1970s and 1980s before his death from AIDS film in 1992. A 2010 exhibit at the Smithsonian's National Portrait Gallery included a Wojnarowicz film that became controversial for its depiction of ants crawling over a crucifix. "It became a cause celeb for the avante garde."

It also was a publicity coup for Fales. "We were very happy that we had been associated with this event," Taylor jokes. "We've been holding the torch for David Wojnarowicz's work for many years now. That's what we collect: the work that pisses people off. It's New York; this work was all done on the Lower East Side."

Meetings

"I probably spend 75 percent of my time trying to get people to give us stuff," Taylor says, "So I'm constantly meeting with potential donors."

Preservation

Located in the Bobst Library along with Fales is the Barbara Goldsmith Preservation Laboratory, with state of the art equipment, according to Taylor. Fales is thus fortunate to take advantage, without cost, of the lab's facilities for bookbinding, full conservation of early books, tape removal, and video and audio reformatting.

ROSENBACH MUSEUM & LIBRARY

We spoke with Librarian Elizabeth E. Fuller, who has been with the Rosenbach for 24 years, and Judith Guston, curator and director of collections, who has been in her job 12 years.

General Description

The Rosenbach Museum & Library, housed in two adjoining townhouses on Delancey Place in Philadelphia's Rittenhouse-Fitler historic district, bills itself as an "internationally known destination for lovers of literature, art, and history." The Rosenbach, named for its founders, Dr. A.S.W. Rosenbach (1876-1952) and his brother, Philip (1863-1953), maintains diverse collections encompassing rare books, manuscripts, furniture, silver, paintings, prints, drawings, and sculpture.

These objects are housed in a hybrid institution that is half-museum and half-library. Though unusual, this scenario is not unique—another example of a hybrid is New York's Morgan Library & Museum.

History and Scope of the Collections

The Rosenbach Museum & Library was founded in 1954 through a testamentary gift by the Rosenbach brothers, who were well known dealers in books, manuscripts, and fine art. The brothers' personal collection comprises the core of the Rosenbach and features such treasures as the only surviving copy of Benjamin Franklin's first *Poor Richard Almanac* and the manuscript of James Joyce's *Ulysses*. The collection has grown to include the papers of poet Marianne Moore, Bram Stoker's notes for *Dracula*, and the drawings of children's author/illustrator Maurice Sendak, among other rare and valuable documents.

The Rosenbach brothers' original residence—the 1865 townhouse at 2010 Delancey Place—is listed on the National Register of Historic Places. The adjacent townhouse, known as the Maurice Sendak Building, opened to the public in 2003 and offers spaces for public programs and exhibitions.

Always on view are selections from the James Joyce, Marianne Moore, and Maurice Sendak collections. Another big draw are the museum's decorative and fine arts collections, containing items that range from Egyptian sculpture and English furniture to American portraiture, an 18th century Philadelphia tall chest, silver by Hester Bateman and Myer Myers, and the largest collection of oil-on-metal portrait miniatures in the United States.

Further highlights of the collections include more than 600 letters from Lewis Carroll; a rare copy of Cervantes' first edition of *Don Quixote*; the largest surviving portions of Charles Dickens' manuscripts for *Pickwick Papers* and *Nicholas Nickleby*, manuscripts for Joseph Conrad's *Lord Jim*, *Nostromo*, and *The Secret Agent*; Dylan Thomas' manuscript for *Under Milk Wood*—and much more.

Americana is a focus of the library—especially the European exploration and settlement of the New World and the political and military history of the United States. These histories are reflected in explorers' and travelers' descriptions of the land and its peoples; maps; broadsides; newspapers; and scriptures, liturgical, and devotional works for the use of Christian missionaries and converts—many in Native American languages. The collections also include Indian treaties and captivity narratives; collections of legal and church documents from the Oregon Territory and colonial Mexico and Peru; and the writings of such figures as Cortéz and Pizarro; George Washington and Ben Franklin; John Adams and Thomas Jefferson; and Abraham Lincoln.

Judaica, medieval manuscripts and books printed before 1500 are among the collection's other, diverse elements.

The Rosenbach's collection of paintings includes important American portraits by Gilbert Stuart, Thomas Sully, Bass Otis, Matthew Jouett, and John Wesley Jarvis; and European genre paintings attributed to Angelica Kauffman and the American expatriate Benjamin West.

"We're a hybrid institution," says librarian Elizabeth E. Fuller. "We're a research library and we're a museum, just as our founders' business was a single company that dealt in rare books and manuscripts and fine and decorative arts. Locally, to people who just walk in the door to see exhibitions, we're best known as a museum, and that's how most of our marketing is viewed.

"Internationally we're better known as a research library. We have the strengths of both--two sets of professional practices to draw from. In practice very often the library and curatorial departments are part of a single collections department; all the staff work very closely together on all aspects of the collection."

Commenting on the Rosenbach's dimensions, Curator Judith Guston says, "Our collection is largely library based because that's where the largest number of things resides." Fuller adds that the overall collection is now near 400,000 objects. "We generally describe it as 30,000 books and for public consumption we say 300,000 pieces of manuscript," she says.

In terms of staff, Fuller is the sole staff member in the library department, but she emphasizes her "close collegial relationship" with the museum's staff of eighteen. The collections department by itself claims five of those staffers. Rosenbach has also had a full-time paraprofessional library assistant in the past, though this position is currently vacant. As librarian, Fuller attends to cataloguing and research inquiries. As curator, Guston oversees the allied tasks of preservation and exhibitions.

Fuller emphasizes that the 1860s townhouse is also "part of the collection," while Guston adds that the collection's materials are those that the Rosenbach brothers "collected and loved" and both owned and sold. Of the two founders, A. S. W. Rosenbach was the more central to the library collection, while Philip concentrated on art and antiques, the women explain. "There are two principal areas of strength in the library collection," Fuller says. "The most broad and diverse segment is American history up to the Civil War; Philip, the older brother, was born during the Civil War. English literature is the other greatest strength of the collection.

"Rosenbach came by his American historical interest as a lifelong Philadelphian whose ancestors had been here since the Revolution. His academic background was in English literature."

Acquisitions and Development

The Rosenbach Museum & Library has a development staff which at full capacity has three persons. There is an endowment for the entire museum, which includes a segregated acquisitions fund for collections. The latter is currently at about half a million dollars. Generally the staff identifies items they wish to purchase and seek targeted funds. In terms of support organizations, the Rosenbach has an upper level membership circle as well as the Delancey Society—plus various other member levels.

Objects are donated "from everywhere," the two staffers say: from attics, from strangers and from long-time associations. Sometimes the library/museum purchases items from these sources. Other purchases come from book dealers and auctions, though there is no distributed wish list.

Ground rules for donations include a signed deed of gift, which assures that the donor has the rights free and clear to the object and that the donation has no strings attached. Encumbrances are rarely agreed to.

Security

Bags and containers are prohibited; pencils and laptops, plus research-related papers (inspected before and after), are allowed. Cameras are not permitted. The small size of the reading room allows easy surveillance.

In modern times, theft has not been a problem, but the library still has "a number of security features in place," says Guston, declining to elaborate.

For requests of photographs of objects, the Rosenbach staffers provide the images and photocopies themselves.

Digitization

Digitization has begun and the library/museum has collaborated with other institutions in this mission. But digitization is not the main priority.

"We're not one of those places that believe in digitizing everything just to get us up online," Fuller explains. "We're careful about how we invest in digitization because we like our digitized materials to be very rich for researchers from off site. Toward that end, the museum/library has built a sub-site titled "Manuscripts Online" where it has posted papers related to George Washington and another Declaration of Independence signer, Robert Morris, as well as Abraham Lincoln. Each manuscript online has been transcribed and can be searched. Papers related to Ben Franklin will be added in the summer of 2011. "We're just hoping it grows," Fuller says.

Collaborative partners in digitization have included the national library of Israel, which has worked with the Rosenbach to digitize Hebrew manuscripts; and the Rylands Library at the University of Manchester in England, which digitized the Rosenbach's Chaucer materials.

Also online is a portion of the library's catalogue: featured there are books from the Marianne Moore collection and thumbnail images from the fine arts collection. Overall, the online catalogue remains a work in progress.

Outreach and Publicity

The library makes use of a staffer who performs marketing duties along with an outside publicist who oversees press contacts and assistance to reporters writing about the Rosenbach's exhibitions.

Projects with collaborative partners are also key. An unusual use of new media was a recent project with Groupon.com, the online discount site. Guston calls it an "extremely successful venture.

"We decided to try a half-price ticket on Groupon," she explains. "We didn't know how many people to expect, and we got 703 people to respond [to the offer to buy open-ended tour tickets] within the given 48 hours, and that's huge." Guston suggests that using Groupon for a specific program or series might also work well.

The Rosenbach is trying social media initiatives, as well, using Twitter, Facebook, and blogs as promotional tools. Blogs have been useful for publicizing the library/museum's ongoing Civil War sesquicentennial anniversary exhibits (which in turn range from the start of the war to postwar history). Collections items featured include newspaper clippings, diaries, and telegraphs, to soldiers' letters home and drawings from abolitionist

John Brown's trial. The items posted online change constantly to reflect individual items' own anniversaries.

Exhibits

The Rosenbach has about seven exhibitions a year and all do well, Guston says.

Current exhibits include "The Civil War Begins" and another commemorating James Joyce's days in Paris. The Rosenbach also annually celebrates Joyce's masterpiece, *Ulysses*, with "Bloomsday," on June 16. The famous book is read aloud in the street over a span of seven hours.

Bloomsday is promoted as the only international holiday in recognition of a work of art.

Meetings

Fuller attends the American Library Association rare book division meeting each year as well as the overall ALA meeting.

Preservation

Preservation is the focus of an annual summertime training for the staff; employees are required to attend, and a different aspect about care and handling is discussed each time, Fuller says.

Protective measures for collections items are handled off-site. "We're very fortunate that we are just a few blocks away [from] the Conservation Center for Art and Historic Artifacts, which is our regional conservation center," Fuller says. The center works on books, manuscripts and other works on paper.

Collaboration

According to Fuller, collaboration with other institutions has been central to the library/museum. The Greater Philadelphia Cultural Alliance is an umbrella group for 300 organizations that offers a jobs bank, collaborative marketing, and group insurance and pension plans. The Rosenbach is also a member of the Philadelphia Area Consortium of Special Collections Libraries, which encompasses 33 libraries—including academic, museum, church-based, historic, and independent libraries. Over the past two decades, the consortium has received several million dollars for cataloguing efforts as well as professional development, and the Rosenbach shares in these resources as well as the networking and inter-organizational opportunities the consortium provides.

Finally, the Rosenbach is an active lender to other organizations' exhibitions, and that can be helpful in the area of preservation, because any borrowing institution is required to underwrite any preservation needed before an object can travel.

An example is the loan last year of Emily Dickinson materials to the New York Botanical Garden, which then funded the conservation of a valuable letter in the Dickinson collection. Such loans are a great marketing tool, Guston says. "It's a great way for [exhibition-goers in other cities] to go home and look us up on the web and see who we are."

CUSHING MEMORIAL LIBRARY AND ARCHIVES, TEXAS A&M UNIVERSITY

We spoke with Dr. J. Lawrence Mitchell, interim director of Texas A&M's Cushing Memorial Library and Archives. Mitchell comes from the university's professorial ranks: He started out at A&M in1989 as head of the English Department. In 2008, he became interim head of Hispanic Studies. In January 2011 he became interim director of the Cushing Library. "I'm a kind of a utility fielder," he jokes.

General Description

Texas A&M, located in College Station, Texas, is that state's first public institution of higher education. The original college was created in 1871 under the auspices of the Morill Act, approved by Congress in 1862 and designed to set up institutions of higher learning whose "leading object shall be, without excluding other scientific and classical studies, and including military tactics, to teach such branches of learning as are related to agriculture and mechanic arts." Hence, the "A&M" in the university's title.

The college modernized in the 1960s, making the "A" and "M" in its name merely symbolic. It also diversified its student body; admitting women and minorities. And participation in the college's Corps of Cadets was made voluntary. Today, the former college is a university, with a student body of over 49,999 and a 5,200-acre campus, making it one of the nation's largest institutions of higher learning.

It retains its strong links to the military as one of only six senior military colleges.

Cushing Memorial Library and Archives has existed as a dual-function special collections library since 1998. Before that, the special collections were housed in the main Sterling B. Evans Library, but Cushing was the first freestanding library on campus. The building was constructed in 1930 and by the late 1960s began to expand. In 1968 the Sterling C. Evans became the main campus library; Cushing was then attached to it.

Cushing itself, meanwhile, was gutted and refurbished, with a beautiful interior built to house the special collections and archives.

Today, literature is a main focal point at Cushing; other major interests are military materials, Western Americana, and the Mexican colonial period. The library employs 17 full-time staff, a regular part-timer, and various part-time students.

When the newly removed building opened, Cushing had 120,000 books; today, Mitchell estimates that this number has grown to 285,000 books, with a manuscript and archives collection that has increased from 14,000 to 22,000 linear feet. Also at Cushing are 500,000 prints, pictures, postcards, photographs, slides, and transparencies, up from

112,000 such items counted in 1998. A recent catalog celebrated this growth with the title "A Decade of Promise: Ten Years of Collecting"

The Collections

Cushing is particularly proud of two major holdings: the Kipling Collection, containing first editions, early materials from India, and letters; and the John Donne Collection, containing all editions of the sixteenth century (1572-1631) poet's work. A collaboration with Texas A&M's Department of English created the Donne Dariorum Project), containing manuscripts and written items dating back to 1633.

Also at Cushing is an extensive Walt Whitman Collection, under the auspices of the French collector Roger Asselineau (1915-2002) and a Mexican Colonial Collection, containing 1,300 volumes and documents related to Texas's colonial Mexican period. Primeros Libros is an "incunabula" ("from the cradle") collection dating from 1501 to 1600. Also in the Spanish mode is the Cervantes Collection, featuring items from Spanish playwright, novelist and poet Miguel de Cervantes.

Recently acquired is the Garnett Family Collection, from the family of Russian translator Constance Clara Garnett (who introduced English speakers to Tolstoy, Dostoevsky, and Chekov); the family also spawned well-known various publishers, novelists, and the founder of the Nonesuch Press.

Another significant holding is the Krueger Collection of art, containing majestic scenes of scenes in the West, and including paintings by Frederic Remington. "We've got more art on campus probably than anyone else," Mitchell boasts; he also mentions the Robert Dawson 18th century French Collection, containing: 15,000 to 18,000 books and paintings centered on the French Revolution; and the Kelsey Americana Collection of bird books and Western Americana.

One rather unusual collection is devoted to Ku Klux Klan materials; it was begun in 1966 to teach students about racism. The collection, now titled American Nativism, has a curator who is both a black American and a Muslim.

Development

For development tasks, the Cushing depends on a development staffer appointed for all A&M libraries. Endowments at the special collections library currently total about a million dollars, Mitchell says, and include a generous one from the Kelsey Collection donors whose funding allows the purchase of significant volumes on American Indians.

A Friends of the Sterling C. Evans Library exists; Cushing does not have a support organization of its own. However, the special collections library does oversee a popular annual fund-raising workshop devoted to book history. Each year in May, the public is invited to learn how to create a physical book from setting its type to making its paper-- "the whole range of the production of a small book," Mitchell says. Even a replica of the English Common Press is used. The workshop attracts about twenty participants a year, paying $150 apiece.

Procurement and Purchasing

"I know a lot of the dealers and I know a lot about collections," Mitchell says, citing a primary reason he was tapped to take over as Cushing's interim director. "If [dealers] know we're collecting in a particular area, they will notify us. There's a dealer in Philadelphia who specializes in Mexican colonial stuff. So any time he gets something, he lets us know and we let him know if we're interested. He'll think of us as the first people to go to."

Donations from estates are accepted "from time to time," Mitchell says. "Some are modest and some are bigger." If estates wish to donate full collections, "We don't necessarily accept everything that's offered to us—if it doesn't fit within our collecting areas we don't really want to take it.

"All libraries these days—special collections and museums—are having the problem of deciding 'how much can we afford to take?'"

All donors must sign a deed of gift, giving the library control over donated materials.

Mitchell says the Cushing also receives catalogues from dealers and buys occasionally at auction. The library does not put out wish lists. "I'm not that great a believer in wish lists because that always makes things more expensive," the librarian comments.

In response to a question, he says that Cushing "rarely" competes with the University of Texas-Austin's larger special collections library, Harry Ransom Center. "They're going after whole collections," Mitchell explains. "In some cases we overlap; they've got something of everything. They were collecting very early on, so in the Garnett family, my own area, they have very early material: letters, manuscripts, and so on. The same [occurs] with the John Cooper Powys family [collection[. [Ransom has] got a lot of primary material, where we've got stuff that tends to complement rather than compete with them."

Mitchell adds that some of the Cushing's acquisitions are built on personal relationships, and those were certainly at play in its acquisition of the Ragan military collection.

"Because of the military background of the institution, people interested in military history will often approach us with materials.

"During World War II, [Texas A&M] claimed, perhaps with some justification, that it produced more officers than West Point and the other [service academies] combined, and there are still a lot of officers trained here."

Connected to the university's military connections, Cushing recently acquired a World War I collection built around the works of Wilfred Owen and purchased from the biographer of the famous British poet and soldier.

A related anecdote tells how, having just completed work on the 1960 film *The Alamo*, actor John Wayne presented the library with a major painting of that historic event—in exchange for an "Aggie" saber. Says Mitchell: "He referred to [the university] as 'the best military institution in the country.'"

Pre-screening and Security

Mitchell calls security at the library "a big issue," and says Cushing had an audit about a year ago. "Interestingly, the main issue was access by faculty and staff to the special collections themselves, which has been unlimited, the director explains. "We have cameras everywhere, but people had keys that got them into their office and also got them into the collections. We're changing that and moving to a swipe card system to get access."

To date Cushing has had no problem with theft, "But of course it's well known that there are lots of enterprising thieves out there. It's also known that approximately 25 percent of theft is internal," Mitchell points out.

In terms of prevention, laptops and pencils are the only carry-in items allow. Photos generally are not generally a problem, but the library does offer the use of its scanners and copiers, depending on the nature and condition of the material. "In many cases we'll say, 'no you can't do that.' People for the most part, even scholars--maybe especially scholars who use special collections—don't know how to handle books."

Digitization

Cushing Library this spring is starting its first round of digitization. A team of staffers has been assembled and trained, Mitchell says, and the first project is the library's most popular items: the archives of the university yearbook and student newspaper. The task is a big one, considering that the yearbook dates back to 1896 and the newspaper almost as long.

"The scanning of them and digitizing in some ways is the easy part," Mitchell says. The hard part is writing the metadata that will allow searches of the material digitized; a librarian must perform that function.

Another priority area is theses and dissertations. Most of the latter already have been microfilmed by UMI, now called ProQuest. But the library is now taking on masters' theses. The problem there is space: the library is at 90 percent capacity. So much of this material will be moved to a remote location that is being built; another remote location is already ready in Austin and will become operational this summer.

The fourth priority is the library's World War I postcard collection; digitization of that collection should happen this summer.

Outreach and Publicity

Mitchell describes internal frustration at Cushing about a new effort by the university that is directly affecting the library's website. "They're trying to 'brand' the university at the moment, and they've constrained the ways in which we can put up information," the director says, "so none of us is very satisfied with the website at the moment…it doesn't get everything."

Curators, Mitchell explains, are unhappy that the university wants a branding identity, with "one color, one typeface and directions [put up on the website] in a particular way." This produces problems such as a search tool that leads only to the larger Sterling catalog and makes a Cushing holdings search confusing.

"There are some technical problems of that sort and the ability to get things up when we're putting on an exhibition," Mitchell says. "We can't always do it as fast as we'd like".

Other than the website issues that limit outreach, the library's archival material is where most of the action is, says Mitchell, primarily due to the archives' heavy use. Besides the university's yearbook, student newspaper, and other items, the archives include papers of former governors and other politicians. Currently there is little publicity about these holdings aside from the information put into the library catalogue, he says. "What we're trying to do in terms of collaboration is work with other institutions within the Texas A&M university system—there are lots of other schools that don't have the resources we have but would like to have access.

"By digitizing them on one hand and by doing fairly extensive finding aids on the other, we can make them aware of what's here.

To bring the public in, the director says, the library offers elegant publications for exhibitions and other events. These may be widely disseminated: a recent catalogue on the

Cervantes Collection is being distributed to institutions with an interest in Spanish materials.

Exhibits

In 2014 Cushing will put on a major World War I exhibit. A current exhibition focuses on the Al Lowman collection's materials from El Paso printer and book designer Carl Hertzog. The collection documents fine printing, book design, and the history of books and printing in Texas, the Southwest, and nationally and internationally.

Meetings

Mitchell will attend the Rare Books and Manuscripts Section of the American Library Association annual meeting this summer. He also plans to attend book sales around the country. "I know many of the major dealers from the West Coast to the East Coast," he says. "Sometimes when you go to a book fair it's a way of seeing what they've got on display.

Preservation

Cushing does as much preservation on site as possible but sometimes outsources items for exhibition. There is no laboratory on-site. If an item is in fragile shape, the library will box it, because the cost of rebinding all the items that need it is prohibitive. "So it's preserving the status quo for the most part," Mitchell says.

UNIVERSITY OF TEXAS AT AUSTIN, HARRY RANSOM CENTER RESEARCH LIBRARY AND MUSEUM

We spoke with Richard Oram, associate director and Hobby Foundation Librarian, who has been with Henry Ransom for 20 years.

General Description

The University of Texas, in the capital city of Austin, was founded in 1883 and is proud of its excellent academic reputation. About 51,000 students are enrolled there, attending 17 colleges and schools and enjoying access to 17 libraries.

One of the more recent and prestigious libraries in UT's system is the Harry Ransom Center, a library-museum described by its founder, Harry Huntt Ransom, in 1956 as "a center of cultural compass...the Bibliothèque Nationale of the only state that started out as an independent nation."

The Center officially opened in 1957 building upon the university's private libraries that dated back sixty years earlier. In 1897, Swante Palm (1815–1899), a Swedish book lover who had immigrated to Austin, gave the university 10,000 volumes from his personal library. Palm's collection of Swedish literature and history was a catch for the institution. But it was not until 1917 that the university really devoted itself to collecting rare books. English professor Reginald Griffith persuaded a UT regent to purchase the library of Chicago businessman John Henry Wrenn. The Wrenn library contained nearly 6,000 first and rare editions of mostly seventeenth- and eighteenth-century English and American authors, in addition to notable manuscripts of the Brontë sisters, Alfred Lord Tennyson, and the Brownings. In 1921 and 1925 came more significant purchases, including a personal library containing all four of the first folio editions of Shakespeare as well as manuscripts and first editions by Lord Byron, Percy Bysshe Shelley, John Keats, and other writers of the Romantic period. The collections were kept at the old library building, now Battle Hall, and later in the rare books library of the Main Building.

The U-T library continued to amass collections for nearly half a century, rising to a million volumes by 1952 and two million by 1968. Credit for this rise belonged to English professor Harry Huntt Ransom, first as dean, then as vice president, provost, president, and finally chancellor of the University of Texas System.

When Ransom established the Humanities Research Center in 1957, he set out to enhance the University's rare book holdings with a new initiative for collection development in the area of rare books and manuscripts. With the acquisition in 1958 of the massive library of Edward Alexander Parsons, consisting of 40,000 volumes and 8,000 manuscripts, Ransom ushered the University into an era of intense collecting.

The Humanities Research Center moved to its current location at 21st and Guadalupe streets on the southwest corner of campus in 1972 and underwent a renovation in 2003, which created a large exhibition space. The building has seven floors of 2,000 square feet each. Presiding over this space and its holdings is a staff of 90, not counting custodians.

The Center's founder, Ransom, died in 1976. In 1978 The Pforzheimer copy of the Gutenberg Bible was purchased in his memory.

Collections

"We never have a problem finding a point of contact with just about anybody," Oram says, of the Center's huge number of holdings.

Books: The Center has more than 800,000 volumes—totaling one of the larger collections in the United States. The breadth of the collection makes possible a study of the history of the printed book from its beginnings to the present day. Incunabular holdings include the Gutenberg Bible of 1454-55, the only complete copy between the two coasts. The Center's copy, on paper, is one of only five complete books in the Western Hemisphere. Other strengths include the Pforzheimer Library of English Literature, early editions of Shakespeare (including three First Folios), seventeenth- and eighteenth-century English periodicals, eighteenth-century English books, the history of science, Victorian novels, little magazines, and the libraries of important authors.

Nineteenth century holdings include items from the Romantic poets, the Rubáiyát of Omar Khayyám, Lewis Carroll, and Walt Whitman. Author collections from 1901 on include Samuel Beckett, John Fowles, James Joyce, D.H. Lawrence. T.E. Lawrence, Norman Mailer, Ezra Pound, George Bernard Shaw, Evelyn Waugh and more.

Manuscripts: The Center has 37,000 linear feet of manuscripts.

Art: The art collection spans the fifteen through twentieth centuries and includes over 65,000 original artworks from the Americas, Europe and Asia. Included are large collections of artworks by British caricaturists George Cruikshank and Max Beerbohm and typographer, engraver, and sculptor Eric Gill. The collection of early modern Mexican art contains paintings, drawings, and prints by Frida Kahlo, Diego Rivera, Miguel Covarrubias, Rufino Tamayo, and José Guadalupe Posada's *Corridos y Calaveras*. The Carleton Lake art collection holds important works by modern French artists and avant-garde drawings by Jean Cocteau. The art collection also holds a significant collection of early twentieth century posters that graphically illustrate the two world wars and the Spanish Civil War.

Film: Included are more than 10,000 scripts for film, television, and radio; more than 15,000 posters, lobby cards, and other advertising materials; and over a million photographs, including film stills, portrait and publicity photographs, set and location reference stills, makeup and wardrobe stills, and candid, behind-the-scenes photographs. The bulk of the collection concerns mainstream Hollywood filmmaking from the silent era through the present day. Hollywood's Golden Age (1930-1950) is particularly well represented. Specific archives include items from and about director David O. Selznick, journalist Mike Wallace, and actors Gloria Swanson, Robert DeNiro, and Zachary Scott.

Photography: The collection has over five million prints and negatives. Included is the first-ever photograph taken from nature, in 1826, by French inventor Nicéphore Niépce.

Development

The Center has a development department of its own with three FTE positions. It also has endowed funds, some targeted, including a Harry Ransom Fund and a directory's discretionary fund.

There is a membership group with multiple tiers--$50 up to $10,000--rather than a "friends of" organization.

Acquisitions

"Our acquisitions are very director-centric here," Oram says, "so most of the larger ones are done by [director] Tom Staley." There are also five curators, including Oram (books), who specialize in various areas and oversee acquisitions.

The Center has relationships with "a small handful," fewer than five, dealers, from whom it consistently acquires new materials. But catalogs and "plenty of offers from all and sundry" are also considered.

Donations from estates are accepted but are usually on the small size—"it has not been our most prevalent mode of acquisition," Oram says, citing UT's status as a younger institution with fewer alumni who collect books. "Historically we have tended to acquire more through state funds," Oram says.

The Center has a standard deed of gift and requires control over physical materials. Few copyrights have been acquired—probably no more than six or seven, Oram says.

Patron use of the Harry Ransom Center has remained stable, at about 6,000 users a year, the librarian says. Space is an issue. Some lesser-used collections will likely be sent to off-site storage shared with the university libraries, says Oram.

Security

New users are asked to present a photo ID and watch an orientation video. Then they register, often online, using the fairly new Aeon system, a tracking/registration/circulation system for special collections. Harry Ransom was one of the first large libraries to use it. (Texas A&A also uses the system.) Aeon allows patrons to request materials, using finding aids and databases, which are linked to it. "It's kind of like a Chinese menu. You can click check boxes on the web and order items that way," Oram says. Aeon is also a tracking system which lets the Center and patrons alike know what materials each patron has used.

Photo duplication by patrons traditionally has not been allowed, but, "We decided we were out of step with the rest of the world," Oram says. So, starting in April 2011, users can take research photos for personal use "with a long set of conditions about handling" and help setting up the photograph. Oram concedes that there will no way to prohibit materials from being put up on the web, but "Other special collections, the large ones, are doing this already, so we will see how it works."

For duplication, the Center for three years has had a copy operation that produces only digital pdfs but no photocopies. "Right now we're retaining everything that we shoot," the librarian says. "So if someone wants something again, we'll just bring it up again and turn it into a pdf and send it to them." (Larger orders are sent on CD.) New orders take two days to several weeks to digitize.

Digitization

Harry Ransom has been digitizing for ten years and eliminated photocopies three years ago, Oram says. To date, the Center has probably amassed 500,000 digitized images, with "less than one percent" on its website, due in part to copyright restrictions on modern and contemporary archival materials. "It's different from a historic archive, Oram says. "With literary figures they usually have estates with lawyers and cease and desist letters."

Digitization is handled by a team, with a staff member creating the metadata. A new asset in this area is a recently hired digitization librarian, who will oversee programs, what is put on the web, and how files are preserved and migrated. "It's such an important area for our future that we thought we needed [this position]," Oram says. Also to be decided in the near future, he says, is which digital asset management system (DAMS) to purchase. A private donor has already offered to underwrite the purchase.

Outreach and Publicity

The Center, in contrast to most special collections, has two FTEs plus volunteers and interns devoted to the area of free (press/broadcast) publicity. Two more FTEs do marketing work, buying ads and producing print deliverables—invitations, keepsakes for exhibitions, mailings to members, and programs.

A lack of funding has made full-scale catalogues a rarity, Oram says. "They're very expensive [but] one big, big exception in size and weight would be a catalogue of our big, historical photography collection, called the Gernsheim Collection; we produced a big, really gorgeous catalogue with the UT press about six months ago."

Nearly all public events are free of charge at the Center. "We certainly don't make money on our programming," Oram says, adding that the library's budget comes from the university and ultimately the state. "Tom Staley has actively pursued fundraising with smaller foundations." The Mellon Foundation and National Endowment for Humanities have been generous donors and a new grant is covering the Center's cataloguing.

Harry Ransom is active in social media and has used Groupon to promote a half-price membership deal. It has also done targeted PR: Six months ago, the Center put out a press release, picked up by the Associated Press, asking the public to help conserve the original *Gone with the Wind* dresses. "Within two weeks we had over $30,000 contributed," Oram says.

Partnerships include sponsorships by large firms for special events and vendors who have donated in-kind items such as food and beverages. UT's central Perry-Castañeda Library provides infrastructure, such as the university catalogue, and has partnered on acquisitions.

Finally, while fellowships are not unusual for a large special collections library, Harry Ransom has an unusually large program: 55 fellows each year, mostly scholars who work on their own research for one to three months under a stipend and reimbursement of some expenses. The Center also offers eight fellowships a year to students writing dissertations.

Exhibitions

A popular current exhibit focuses on writer David Foster Wallace (1962-2008), author of *Infinite Jest* (1996), *The Broom of the System* (1987), *Girl with Curious Hair* (1989), and numerous collections of stories and essays..

Another current and centenary exhibit revolves around the archive from playwright Tennessee Williams (1911-1983), who wrote such classics as *The Glass Menagerie* (1945) and *A Streetcar Named Desire* (1947).

Events are also being planned to celebrate the 35th anniversary of the film *All the President's Men*, concerning the Watergate scandal. A panel with actor-director Robert Redford and journalists Bob Woodward, and Carl Bernstein will be featured.

A 2010 exhibit using the Center's extensive film collections was titled *Making Movies*. Another that year, called *Viva! Mexico's Independence*, marked the 200th anniversary of Mexico's independence from Spain and the 100th anniversary of the Mexican Revolution.

Meetings

The Center's archivists typically attend Society of American Archivists meetings, while the librarians attend the Rare Books and Manuscripts Section of the American Library Association.

Preservation

Harry Ransom does most of its own preservation, using its own book, photography, and paper laboratories. Seven conservators are on staff. Among the resources they have on the premises is an unusual mold removal chamber, with a special exhaust feature to protect workers.

The Center uses outsourcing "almost never" and even handles its own book-binding, Oram says.

AMERICAN MUSEUM OF NATURAL HISTORY LIBRARY

We spoke with Tom Baione, the Harold Boeschenstein director of library services, American Museum of Natural History. Baione, a librarian, has held his position a year and has been with the AMNH library since 1995.

The American Museum of Natural History (AMNH) was founded in 1869, thanks to the efforts of naturalist Albert Bickmore who lobbied intensely for a natural history museum in New York. With support from powerful supporters such as Theodore Roosevelt, Sr., father of the 26th U.S. president; J. Pierpoint Morgan; and then-Governor John Thompson Hoffman, a legislative bill was passed and a charter created. When the museum finally opened, its first home was the Central Park Arsenal.

The new institution, however, quickly outgrew that first locale, so land was purchased across from Central Park between 77th and 81st streets. A cornerstone for the new building was laid in 1874 and the museum reopened in 1877.

The original Victorian Gothic building was designed by Calvert Vaux and J. Wrey Mould, architects of Central Park, but that building was eclipsed by the museum's south range, a neo-Romanesque brownstone designed by J. Cleaveland Cady. The Beaux-Arts monument entrance on Central Park West, which became the New York State memorial to Theodore Roosevelt, leads to a basilica famous for its rearing Barosaurus. The 77th Street foyer is just as famous for its Haida canoe and is adjacent to the oldest extant museum exhibit on Northwest Coast Indians. The Rose Center and Planetarium opened in 2000.

AMNH boasts an annual attendance of five million and is widely considered as a "must-see" for visitors to New York.

The Library

Founded in 1869 as part of the museum's charter, the Library gathered its book and serial collections through gifts, including the John C. Jay Library on Conchology, the Carson Brevoort Library on Fishes and General Zoology, the Ornithological Library of Daniel Giraud Elliot, the Harry Edwards Entomological Library, the Hugh Jewett collection of Voyages and Travel, and the Jules Marcou Geology Collection. In 1903 the American Ethnological Society located its library at AMNH as well, and in 1905 the New York Academy of Sciences also deposited its collection of 10,000 volumes there.

Today, the Library maintains a staff of 14.5 FTE and is one of the largest natural history libraries in the world, spanning all categories of the natural sciences except for botany. It also includes the Museum's astronomy collection, transferred from the Hayden Planetarium in 1997.

The Library, located on two floors of one building and eight stories of another, states that its primary function is to serve and support the work of the Museum's scientific staff. The public is invited to use the Library three-and-a-half hours three afternoons a week, free of the museum admission fee. Other parts of the library—special collections storage and rare books—normally are open to museum and Library staff only.

The Special Collections

Baione estimates that the AMNH Library holds about 600,000 volumes, but calls the volume issue "a tricky one because we haven't been binding for nearly ten years."

The Special Collections, which are contiguous with but sequestered from the rest of the Library, include archival material relating to the history of the Museum, its scientists and staff, expeditions and research, exhibitions, education, and general administrative history. Special Collections uses four FTE of the Library's overall staff.

The Rare Book and Rare Folio collection now numbers more than 14,000 books relevant to natural history, field diaries and scrapbooks; illustrated, fragile or uniquely bound materials; limited and/or autographed editions; published and unpublished materials with a special Museum association; and materials of high monetary value.

Importantly, however, rare books and journals are *not* part of the Special Collections. "What we consider 'rare books' are still used as tools by scientists," Baione explains. "The way we see it organizationally, [rare books and journals are] part of the [duties of the] reference librarian for the book and journal collection."

The Special Collections do include photography, moving images, art, archives and manuscripts, memorabilia and a category called "realia," which Baione says may include items created for short-term exhibition or educational purposes, such as architectural models or pieces of scientific equipment. Though zoological specimens are kept elsewhere in the scientific departments, a canary that a respected Museum taxidermist preserved when he was only age ten is included with his individual memorabilia in Special Collections.

The Special Collections photographic collection includes about one million images; a moving image collection of 291 cataloged titles; and thousands of other films and video tapes. Copies of some of the entries to the annual Margaret Mead Film and Video Festival are found in Special Collections as well.

Among the Collections' treasures are books dating back to the 1400s. Among the 1500s books are works by Italian scientist Ulysses Aldrovandi and his Swiss teacher Conrad Gesner. There is a first edition of Charles Darwin's *The Origin of Species* plus a page of the original manuscript. There is a full set of John James Audubon's *Birds of America* as well as reports from important voyages and explorations. Among the latter is the U.S.

Exploring Expedition 1838-41, the nation's first seagoing exploration. The zoologist on board, Titian Ramsey Peale, painted Kilauea volcano in Hawaii plus other scenes from the expedition. Another item from the expedition is a log from the *Peacock* recording what is believed to be the first documented sighting of Antarctica.

Development

The Library has no development person or "Friends of" organization of its own but instead underwrites its expenses and most of its acquisitions via its budget from the Museum.

The Library also participates in behind-the-scenes events for museum members. One event this year, sponsored by the Junior Committee for members, focused on the Library treasures, and another, called "Science at Work," also focused on the Library, inviting patrons to an intimate tour and talk . Such events reinforce the Library's existence and importance, Baione says: "We were able to show them how we were using new tools we had created in our archives to help us do research about non-archival materials in our collections."

Otherwise, the Library is free to seek its own foundation or government funding with assistance from the Museum's development staff. It also has endowment funds targeted for such acquisitions as books on mammals and items related to the polar regions—their native Inuit people and, geology, instance. The largest endowment, says Baione, funds his own position and comes from the Boeschenstein family in memory of their father, Harold, a Museum trustee.

Acquisitions

The Library's Collection Management Policy is currently under review. The policy lists all subjects the Museum considers relevant to its mission. "We don't try to collect everything," Baione points out. Library of Congress subject headings in the policy clarify what is desired and what is forwarded elsewhere.

If an item related to botany is offered, for instance, or an item related to domesticated animals, the Museum will likely pass on the donation or refer the donor to another institution, such as the New York Botanic Garden in the Bronx.

In other parts of the Museum, there is a formal accession policy; in the Library, any first edition with a call number may be accepted as a replacement for a damaged book.

Security

Photos with personal cameras are permitted—without tripods or flash. The availability of a walk-up scanner allows a patron to place the desired book image face-up on the scanner bed and operate a touch screen interface made by Digital Library Systems Group. The scanner is a KIC (Knowledge Information Center). Such image equipment is "devised to make it really easy," Baione says. "A user can choose a format of file they need once their scanning is complete--a pdf, a searchable pdf, a TIFF or JPEG--and capture it on a thumb drive or send it via email."

"It's neat because it saves lots of paper," Baione continues. "People just don't make photocopies anymore". Staffers, he says, are so pleased that they have requested the purchase of a second scanner. "We have lots of other pieces of scanning equipment, but this is the first one that people can just walk up to and use," the librarian observes.

In terms of security, "We're an extremely secure part of the museum. We have multiple safes and we have rare book and other rare-materials enclosures in the stacks that have many layers of redundant security systems. We have biometric security features—using iris or fingerprint scanning material--and the [list of] staff allowed to access secure areas is short."

Digitization

The assistant director for library acquisitions manages library serial publications, which now are almost entirely electronic. "We don't subscribe to anything in print if there's an electronic version," Baione says. To read materials, Library users can employ anything from the AMNH website to tablets to cell phones. Articles from outside journals and articles as well as the four scientific journals the Library publishes are freely available as pdfs.

In coming months, a new experimental format set up for tablet readers, called ePub, will enable readers to enlarge text on pdfs; the Museum publication *American Museum Novitates* will be first to offer readers this capability. A problem with the program is pagination distortion, which the Library hopes to fix soon, Baione says.

Photos are also being digitized; the Library's ownership of original negatives makes scans clearer, makes putting images online easier, and boosts preservation efforts. Volunteers have been a big help on this lengthy project. "We're just going shelf by shelf," Baione says.

Among AMNH's partnerships are a Metro New York library group and the Bioinformation Science Consortium, or BISC.

For digitization of books, the Library is a founding member of the Biodiversity Heritage Library, a group of natural history libraries in the U.S. and U.K. The five-year-old project, an offshoot of the *Encyclopedia of Life* website, aims to create digitized versions of all literature about living organisms, "from a virus to a whale," Baione says. The MacArthur Foundation is a major funder. The AMNH, partnering with the not-for-profit Internet Archive, sends its materials on a book truck to a scanning facility in New Jersey. Only non-rare, non-fragile, non-copyright-protected materials that fit within certain size ranges can be scanned. "We are kind of limited," Baione acknowledges, but points out that "for the first time, literature about remote parts of the world are being 'virtually' repatriated with free online use." Scanner items are marked with paper wrappers advising on-site users that their contents are now online.

The Library is working to spread this online wealth, Baione says: "We're approaching like institutions to say 'It behooves you to provide free access to your scientific output via these journals that you publish. You provide them for free. May we also take copies and provide them through the Biodiversity Heritage Library, where we know a lot of people will look for this stuff and cite it in the future?'"

Overall, he hopes to partner with more open source online projects. He recalls having a staffer prized for his extensive programming experience, but then the staffer left. "We were unable to find anyone who had all those skills and the knowledge of all those languages that allowed this database to function," Baione says. "We had to find something else." Ultimately the Library acquired Omeka, an open-source, free software package that allows an institution to marry its individual customized digitizing procedures to standardized ones.

Omeka members help one another with problems—making the departure of one key staff member no longer a crisis. Says Baione: "We learned an important and expensive lesson."

Outreach and Publicity

The Museum's website offers changing features on the Library, as does the Museum newsletter, sent to all members. The Library also offers its news on the site along with a RSS feed option for frequent users. These features may concern recent acquisitions and gifts.

Exhibits are not covered, however, since the separate exhibit gallery no longer exists. The former director did away with the exhibition program, believing that it didn't fit with the mission of the Library. "We've had a lot of cuts. It would be hard to justify," Baione acknowledges.

Outreach efforts continue, however. The Library agrees to every request from library schools and other academic institutions for student tours.

Baione, meanwhile, emphasizes that he's still so new "I'm just getting my feet wet" on projects he wants to pursue. But one he envisions, for funding and outreach, would piggyback onto an event the Library does each year for conservation of specific items.

This "adopt a book" project, which Baione saw in action at the Grolier Club Library in New York, would involve presenting attendees with a display of "neediest cases," meaning books needing conservation work. Donors would sign up to "adopt" these books.

Such fund-raising must be done in league with the Museum's development office to avoid overlapping with proposals from other parts of the Museum.

Conservation

The AMNH Library looked to the future when it built the current library facility in 1993. The Library has a full-time conservator and full-service lab, capable of conducting a variety of paper and book conservation. In addition to a fume hood, its own de-ionized water source for washing paper, and extensive collection of bookbinding tools and equipment, the lab offers bench space for up to five conservators simultaneously.

In addition to the full-time conservator, the Library has successfully obtained government and private funding to conserve specific collections of materials, from books and prints to artwork, models, and photographic materials.

WISCONSIN HISTORICAL SOCIETY LIBRARY

We spoke with Dr. Rick Pifer, an archivist and director of public services at the Wisconsin Historical Society's Library-Archives, where he has worked for 20 years.

General Description

The Wisconsin Historical Society, located in Madison, Wisconsin, was founded in 1846, two years before Wisconsin became the 30th state. Eventually the Society became one of the largest and most active state historical societies in the country. A cross between a state agency and a private membership organization, the Society receives 60 percent of its funding from the state and the remaining 40 percent from membership fees, admission fees to its museum, gifts, trust funds, and grants. The Society's mission statement is to help people "connect to the past by collecting, preserving, and sharing stories."

The Library-Archives (hereafter "the Library") is located in the Historical Society headquarters, off State Street in Madison, on the campus of the University of Wisconsin (the Society's Museum is elsewhere.) There are close town-gown ties between these institutions, since the Library-Archives serves as the university's American History Library.

The Library, which is open to the public, occupies four floors plus the additional stack space of the Society.

"We are an unusual critter as historical agencies go," Pifer points out, citing "our association with the University and how long we've been collecting." Both the library and its archives are larger than those of most state historical societies, he points out.

The Society's budget comes primarily from the state, whose $5.2 million annual provision is relatively stable, though budget reductions loom, Pifer says. The Society's employees, including those in the Library, work for the State. However, a foundation run by the Historical Society also supports the Society and Library through the donations of its 13,000 members. "We are both literally a state agency--and an organization that you can 'join,'" Pifer says.

A board of directors, the Board of Curators, appointed by the governor or the legislature or elected by the membership, directs the Society and Library.

The Library-Archives: Background

The Library, which has 43 permanent staffers plus university student workers, has roughly 4 million items and 100,000 cubic feet of archival materials, making it Wisconsin's second largest library after that of U-W. "Essentially we are full," Pifer comments of the space issue; the Library is planning for a major remote storage facility.

The Library serves as the United States-Canadian history collection for the university, so its collections go far beyond the state boundaries of Wisconsin. The Library dates back as far as the Historical Society, because the latter's founders, Pifer says, had the goal of creating "the greatest library of the West," since, at the time, Wisconsin was "the West." From the beginning the founders collected not only published materials but unpublished primary sources as well. The first director, Lyman Draper, "was one of those mid 19th century quintessential collectors," Pifer says. "He was a biographer [and] he was interested in the settlement of the trans-Appalachian West. Throughout he was collecting primary sources that related to the settlement of the early nation, and that not only produces some very rich collections that date back to the colonial period but also really sets the stage for ongoing collecting throughout the 19th and 20th centuries."

The Library-Archives: Collection

The Library's Archives Collection is particularly proud of its genealogy collection, consisting of published and unpublished materials for researching family lineage and history. "We've been collecting genealogy since the latter quarter of the 19th century at least," Pifer says. "We tend to think of ourselves as being in the top five genealogy collections in the country."

The General North American History Collection, also found in the Archives, constitutes the largest collection focused on the nation's history and is comprised of books, microfilms, newspapers and other periodicals, and pamphlets and ephemera. Government Information and Records is a third category and includes government publications by Wisconsin offices and agencies; plus materials from other state governments, the federal government and the Canadian government. The Library's local government records consist of original records from Wisconsin municipalities, school districts, courts, and counties. The Wisconsin State Archives includes original records of the state governor's office and executive agencies, the state legislature, and the state supreme court.

The Manuscript Collections cover the private papers and organization records of various groups and also contain film and theater collections, labor history collections, mass communications collections, the McCormick-International Harvester Collection, the Social Action Collections, and the Trans-Allegheny Frontier.
Other materials in the Archives include over 30,000 maps and atlases documenting North American exploration, economic development, and land ownership. Also in the Archives

are over 2 million photographs and other visual materials documenting Wisconsin and U.S. history.

In terms of specific holdings, "We have what may be the largest newspaper collection outside the Library of Congress," Pifer says. Credit belongs to the Library's recently retired periodicals librarian, James Danky. The collection includes major Native American, African American, and "Underground" (from the Sixties to the present) newspaper collections. Locals consider the Wisconsin institution the "largest freestanding American history library in the country" (since the Library of Congress is not solely a history library).

Other gems within the Archives are major Daniel Boone and Chief Tecumseh collections, and an organized labor collection put together by U-W economists. "We hold the records of the American Federation of Labor up to the point that it merged with the CIO in 1955," Piper says. "We have a significant body of material related to the Teamsters Union, and there are dozens of other unions we have."

Another major national area is mass communications, also begun by a university faculty member; the collection includes the records of the National Broadcasting Company from the radio era through 1955. A social action collection includes materials from the civil rights era in the Mississippi Delta region, the Student Nonviolent Coordinating Committee, the Congress on Racial Equality, and Students for Democratic Society.

Development

The Library-Archives, which is largely supported by the state budget, also makes use of funding from the Society's foundation and its paid membership, as well as from endowed funds. The latter concentrates on genealogical materials. There is no Friends of organization.

Acquisitions

In the Library-Archives, the Archives side has a supervisor of acquisitions and two archival staff—one focused on manuscripts, one on local government records, and two on state government records.

The same supervisor is in charge of the acquisitions staff in the Library, which includes a periodicals librarian, a library acquisitions librarian, and several support staff. Material comes in via gifts, but most acquisition consists of purchases via the acquisitions budget. The Library requires control of any gifts; some copyrights are deeded by donors.

Security

Library users can carry in anything they need with which to take notes, such as laptops, pencils and paper, but they cannot bring in any kind of bag—including laptop bags, purses, backpacks, even fanny packs.

"Our primary [means of] security is that everything is constantly monitored," Pifer says. The archival stacks are controlled by secure doors. The Library stacks are open stacks, however. The Library has suffered two instances of theft, both times internal, but nothing recent.

Photos by patrons' own digital cameras are allowed for research purposes only. Photos for reproduction are available only through an in-house digital lab that does high-grade work at virtually any size and in-house printing up to 24 inches wide. For normal-size images the Library charges seven cents an image on an honor system.

Digitization

"We kind of think we're far along as state historical societies go; we have an active digitization program," Pifer reports. "But I would be surprised if any more than one-tenth of one percent is digital."

Key to the Library's collection digitization is Google. Four years ago, the Society and the University of Wisconsin signed an agreement with the search engine giant to begin the digitization process.

Already that process has digitized the Library's Family History collection, Pifer says. But details are kept cloaked. Shipments from the U-W and the Society regularly are sent out for scanning to a Google-owned facility whose location is kept secret from the public.

"We believe very strongly in the digital future, and digital content that is done by Google gets linked into the catalog," the archivist says. Furthermore, the Library catalog is the same as that of the university system.

A second aspect of digitization is actually a profit center: Eleven years ago, the Library started digitizing photographs and now has 50,000 online on an e-commerce site—linked to the Library's main website. That e-commerce site was built specifically to sell photographs. The cost ranges from $15.50 for a 5-by-7-inch print to $70 for a poster-size prize; prints are sent to users by mail. This business pays for its own operations and returns a profit, Pifer says.

Another profit center is the Wisconsin Genealogical Research Service, in which the Library has mounted its indexes to specific records that patrons can order online or receive as copies.

Yet another digital operation involving library and archives materials is fueling a new civil war site that was scheduled to go live in mid-April in line with the sesquicentennial anniversary of the Civil War. "That site will have roughly 20,000 pages of content," Pifer said. The initial release was to involve a comprehensive site geared to the war's timeline.

How to build digitization into the processing work for manuscripts is a central goal of the archival side of the Library, Pifer says.

Outreach and Publicity

The Library-Archives does not publicize its collections to the research community but instead depends on those individuals hearing about materials at U-W via secondary sources.

Publicity efforts are active, however, in terms of the genealogical community; the Library is working toward a Midwestern marketing campaign to attract people willing to travel to Madison for family research.

Outreach also occurs in tandem with U-W in line with the Library's role as the university's American History Library. One side of this is curricular work with faculty to bring classes in to the Library to examine primary materials.

For younger students statewide, the Library works with the Society's own National History Day staff to help children research primary-source materials and prepare historical presentations for judging at regional, state, and national events.

Meetings

Pifer regularly attends archival meetings with the Midwest Archives Conference and the Society of American Archivists. Other staffers attend Wisconsin Library Association meetings and occasionally American Library Association meetings.

Preservation

The Library-Archives has a preservation coordinator on staff as well as a small lab for paper conservation. The Library also has a conservator for paper preservation, a staffer dedicated to working with Library materials, and a microfilm lab with three staffers. Some conservation and microfilming work is outsourced. Book binding also is outsourced.